Original title:
Shoes of Change

Copyright © 2025 Creative Arts Management OÜ
All rights reserved.

Author: Riley Donovan
ISBN HARDBACK: 978-1-80586-195-9
ISBN PAPERBACK: 978-1-80586-667-1

Carefree Footprints

Silly sandals on my feet,
They squeak and squawk with every beat.
To dance around the grassy ground,
Fun's the only thing I've found.

A pair of flip-flops, loud and bright,
Chasing shadows, what a sight!
With each step, a comet's trail,
I'm off to tell a silly tale!

A Rhythm of Renewal

In quirky clogs, I stomp and prance,
Each step unfolds a funny dance.
With socks that clash and stripes so bold,
My silly style is pure gold!

Unruly sneakers lead the way,
I laugh at puddles, come what may!
The world's a stage, oh what a show,
As I bounce through life, to and fro!

Walking Towards Change

Oh what fun in wobbly shoes,
I trip and tumble, share my views.
Each time I fall, I giggle bright,
Change is just a clumsy flight!

My laces dance, they twist and tie,
Like playful thoughts that soar and fly.
With every step, I leap and bound,
In laughter's grip, life knows no bound!

Strides of Self-Discovery

Bright high-tops with stripes of glee,
Take me where I want to be.
Each stomp a story, every slip,
The joy of life's a vibrant trip!

A little wiggle and a spin,
Change is great, let's dive right in!
With every step, I find my way,
In silly joy, I'll laugh and play!

The Rhythm of New Horizons

Laces dancing in the breeze,
They whizz and whirr with ease.
Each step a jig, a funky beat,
Bounding forth on happy feet.

Old kicks sigh, they had their fun,
While new ones twirl under the sun.
They hold adventures yet untold,
With soles like dreams that never get old.

Marks Left in Dust and Hope

Dusty paths where feet did roam,
Leave behind a quirky poem.
A scuffed toe tells a tale or two,
Of every awkward step we drew.

A print so bold, a splash of flair,
Worn with pride, a little care.
On every trail, we laugh and skip,
With merry hearts, we take our trip.

Boundless Steps, Limitless Aspirations

Strutting down the lane so grand,
Each stomp declares, 'I understand!'
With every twirl, the world's a stage,
We're all the stars at any age.

Flipping flops and squeaky heels,
These quirky styles, oh how they feel!
With bouncy toes, we take a stand,
In mismatched socks, come join the band.

Footprints of Tomorrow's Possibilities

With every step, I tiptoe lightly,
In kicks that shine and fit just rightly.
A skip, a slide, what a delight!
Ready for giggles to take flight.

Tomorrow's options stretch so wide,
While silly prints are our guide.
In shining paths, we chase the fun,
With every stride, we have just begun.

The Kaleidoscope of Movement

In the closet they reside, bright and bold,
Each pair tells a tale, awkward yet gold.
One's got a squeak, another's a flop,
Dance like a penguin, or just make it stop!

Laces tangled like spaghetti on a plate,
One escaped, he thinks he's late for a date.
The sandals whisper, 'We'll bring you cheer,'
While the boots stomp and laugh, 'We have no fear!'

Sneakers zooming, they glide and slip,
While loafers just stare with a dignified tip.
Flip-flops chatter in their breezy tone,
'Catch us if you can, but leave us alone!'

So here's to the steps we trip and fall,
With mismatched patterns, we'll conquer it all.
Through puddles and rainbows, every stride,
Life's a waltz, just glide with pride!

Pathways Unseen

In a world of soles, it's truly absurd,
Every step can leave you feeling stirred.
Strutting in flip-flops, feeling so free,
They must be the reason for the wobbly spree!

High-tops get jealous, they look quite fierce,
While sandals gossip, 'Oh dear, they pierce!'
But who needs fashion when fun's the goal?
Let's fling off the norms, and just roll with the stroll!

Through muddy puddles and fresh spring air,
Chasing your shadow, who really would care?
With each clumsy step, giggles erupt,
Twirling like whirlwinds, in flip-flops or clogs.

So take on the journey, let laughter prevail,
With whimsical footwear, you'll never fail.
On this wobbly path, let joy be your guide,
In mismatched attire, let friendships abide!

Beyond Every Sole

In a closet, chaos reigns,
A shoe army fights for gains.
Sneakers squeak, and heels complain,
Each pair dreams of world-wide fame.

Sandals tease the winter's cold,
Boots tell tales that must be told.
Loafers grumble, feeling old,
While flip-flops dance, bold and gold.

Every sole has a story here,
Of wild nights and morning cheer.
With every step, let's spread the cheer,
In funky footwear, we persevere.

Yet sometimes, they clash and fight,
Argue over wrong and right.
But in the end, all unite,
To take us where the day feels bright.

Revolution in Every Step

A quirky croc slipped on my foot,
Determined to start a fashion loot.
Socks and sandals, what a look!
Revamping the style book, oh what a hook!

In bright red boots, I stride quite proud,
Prancing like I'm in a crowd.
Each stomp makes a thunderous sound,
Who knew fashion could be this loud?

The flip-flops rally in the sun,
Racing to see who is the fun.
With every bounce, they're second to none,
Who says changes can't be done?

A shiny pump got lost last night,
In the dance-off, what a sight!
But here they are, ready to ignite,
Our feet march with sheer delight!

The Path Less Walked

In mismatched boots, I take my route,
Every step's a laugh, no doubt.
High-tops whisper, "Have you seen?"
While loafers dream of being sleek and clean.

Each pathway calls with giggles bright,
Sneakers buzz with sheer delight.
Old sandals shout, "Let's take flight!"
As we strut into the night.

Slippers slide through muddy bends,
Squealing joy at fashion trends.
Though my style may not make sense,
Every step is a wild expense.

In every scuff, a tale unfolds,
With every twist, the journey holds.
Let's dance like the world's our mold,
With laughter echoing, brave and bold.

Journeys Worn with Pride

Here comes a gap-toothed sneaker crew,
With laces tangled in a stew.
Each sprint is filled with clumsy grace,
Creating chaos in their place.

Oh, how the worn-out soles complain,
As I push through puddles, a new terrain.
But every splash brings smiles afresh,
In soggy fun, we've found our mesh.

My sandals squeak under sunny skies,
And wish for quieter lullabies.
Yet in their clatter, a joy flies,
Shared laughter shines, a sweet surprise.

From crocks to boots, we take a ride,
With every quirk, it's fun we bide.
In this parade, let's stand with pride,
For every path, no need to hide!

Tracks of Transition

In sneakers worn, I start my day,
With laces tied in a comical way.
One foot leads, the other just drags,
It's a clumsy dance with awkward swag.

With each step taken, I feel the shift,
A goofy glide, like a playful gift.
I trip on dreams, then bounce and twirl,
In this silly journey, I spin and whirl.

Soles on a New Path

My sandals squeak with every stride,
Like vinyl records on a crazy ride.
I stride with flair, a showman's grace,
While dodging puddles in a fast-paced race.

Each pair I wear comes with a tale,
From squishy flip-flops to boots that sail.
They dance and leap, then trip me up,
I might just need a larger cup!

Footfalls of Freedom

My fluffy slippers glide with ease,
They make me feel like I'm floating on breeze.
I hop and skip in patterned bliss,
How could life be better than this?

With every shuffle, I risk a fall,
But laughter echoes—it's the best of all.
In wacky steps, I find my groove,
These zany kicks make me wanna move!

Progress in Every Step

With boots so big, I stomp around,
Leaving laughter in each clumsy sound.
A waddle here, a glide over there,
Who knew progress could bring such flair?

I dance like nobody's watching me,
While neighbors peek, so curious, you see.
But I'm on a mission, can't be stopped,
In silly strides, my joy just popped!

Soles of Transformation

In funky colors, they dance with glee,
Those silly soles, oh can't you see?
They waddle and wiggle, a sight to behold,
Transforming steps from shy to bold.

A left foot leads, the right just follows,
Together they trip, through giggles and hollows.
Snagged on a rug, they tumble and sway,
Soles of transformation, come join the play!

Steps into Tomorrow

With every step, a fresh debut,
Squeaky like toddlers, how they squeal too!
They skip and hop, in search of fun,
Treading through puddles, oh, what a run!

Old scuffs and stains tell tales untold,
In new adventures, they shimmer like gold.
Who'd thought such fun could stretch for miles?
With each step forward, they echo with smiles!

Heels of Hope

Perched up high, with a feisty cheer,
Wobbling slightly, but never in fear.
They tap, tap, tap like a drum at play,
Heels of hope, will lead the way!

Strutting down the street, a bit of sass,
With every strut, they kick up some grass.
A misstep here, a laugh erupts,
Funky heels, never interrupt!

Tread of Tomorrow

Tread cautiously, oh, the ground is slick,
With laughter and smiles, let's take that risk!
With every slip, a giggle will burst,
The tread of tomorrow, quenching our thirst.

They race on the pavement, in sunshine bright,
Chasing the giggles 'til day turns to night.
Each little blunder, a story we weave,
With a twirl and a glide, it's hard to believe!

The Layers of Movement

On my feet, a rainbow squats,
With soles so bright, they grab the thoughts.
Each step I shuffle, a dance unfolds,
In layers worn, my stories told.

From flip-flops to boots, I change my game,
A waltz in waves, it's never the same.
The more I switch, the more I glide,
With playful steps, I take pride.

With every pair, a giggle returns,
In sneakers high, my spirit churns.
Fashion faux pas? I laugh it away,
Each layer a joke, chasing grays away.

Wayfarers of the New

With laces loose and colors bright,
I tread a path of sheer delight.
Where am I off to, who can say?
These wacky kicks just love to play.

Adventures call, they shout my name,
Each step a giggle, far from tame.
In these clunky pals, I strut around,
In style so weird, I'm homeward bound.

Past puddles and parks, I prance with glee,
New friends I make on this wild spree.
From neon to plaid, every scheme,
With laughter and joy, I chase a dream.

Unraveled Journeys

My sneakers squeak while my heart skips,
Each wobble a dance, as laughter drips.
In untied dreams, I wander wide,
With paths quite twisted, it's quite a ride.

A clown at play, my feet take flight,
In mismatched patterns, a funny sight.
Through ups and downs, I trip and fall,
Yet in these quirks, I stand up tall.

With every misstep, a tale unfurls,
I navigate through this silly world.
In playful strides, I find my groove,
With each new stumble, I start to move.

Fresh Prints of Tomorrow

Tomorrow's steps, so fresh and bright,
I strut the block, in pure delight.
With patterns wild, I can't contain,
These quirky prints drive me insane!

Each sole a map, of trails unknown,
As I teeter and twirl, I'm not alone.
I trip on dreams, with laughter as fuel,
In bright yellow socks, I'm nobody's fool.

From city streets to grassy knolls,
Unruly fun fills up my soles.
In every flip and silly hop,
I find my way, I won't stop!

Footsteps Through Time

In a closet deep and vast,
Old sneakers whisper tales of past.
Each scuff and mark, a tale to tell,
Of adventures that went rather well.

Here's a sandal, lost its pair,
It danced with flair, without a care.
A high heel once, thought it so grand,
Now it hides in the dust, unmanned.

Flip-flops skipped through summer suns,
While boots marched on for winter runs.
They trudge and twirl, they twist and bend,
In a parade where all trends blend.

From clogs to slides, they all confess,
Footloose lives, oh what a mess!
Each step a giggle, a stuttered rhyme,
As we trip through this hurried time.

A Shift Beneath

Slippers snicker in the dark,
As I chase my dogs around the park.
Every stride brings laughter's cheer,
Oh the places my feet hold dear!

Loafers smug with polished pride,
Grumble when I slip and slide.
The runners giggle, swift and sleek,
While I fumble, trip, and squeak.

Mismatched socks play peek-a-boo,
With every jump, they draw a cue.
A hefty boot, just two left feet,
Join the dance, oh what a feat!

Cumbersome loafers, now they're shy,
Hiding when the disco calls to fly.
The stages missed, sighs fill the air,
While I fumble with flair everywhere.

The Dance of Destiny

Ballet flats, and tap shoes too,
Choreographing jobs askew.
A cakewalk in a muddy path,
Was that a slip or just a laugh?

Heels try to spin but fall instead,
While silly slippers play the lead.
With every cha-cha, joy erupts,
As mismatched shoes just erupt!

Kicks of fortune dance around,
Lost in shuffle, never found.
Bouncing left, then right to sway,
Oh look, there goes my shoe bouquet!

So join the twirl, don't be shy,
Even with a loving sigh.
In this gala of feet and fun,
We stumble but still make a run.

Tread Boldly

A quirky jogger meets a heel,
Whispers of boldness in their deal.
Step on cracks and dodge the mud,
While hoping that they won't get stuck!

The shadows of the soles collide,
With echoes of laughter worldwide.
Velcro shoes make a game of it,
While attitude and style just fit.

Flippers flounder, clogs just chime,
Every footstep is a funky rhyme.
As laughter lingers, they take the lead,
In the march of life, all are freed!

With wobbly steps and silly spins,
Together, oh what chaos wins!
In this journey, we find our way,
With every footfall, come what may.

Shoes that Speak

In daylight bright, they dance and prance,
With every step, they take a chance.
Whispers soft, they laugh and sigh,
Oh my dear, how time does fly!

They tell of puddles, joys, and mess,
Of muddy paths and a little stress.
With every creak, they share a tale,
Of wobbly trips and winds that sail.

From cobbled streets to grassy knolls,
They've ventured far, collected souls.
In the closet, they rest at night,
Dreaming of tomorrow's flight!

So let them shine in all their glory,
These funky friends, such a funny story!
When they get together, oh what a show,
Dancing knees high, toe to toe!

Paces of Possibility

Step by step, what will unfold?
Possibilities, bright and bold.
In a world where nothing stays,
A twirl can change the tedium's ways.

Bouncing beats in every stride,
An impromptu jig, oh what a ride!
With soles on fire and lace askew,
Adventure calls, come join the crew!

With every clack, with every clop,
The journey's fun; let's never stop!
Lost in giggles, found in glee,
These paces dance us to be free.

Around the block, then down the street,
Who knew our feet could be so sweet?
Each turn brings laughter, joy, and cheer,
With every step, there's nothing to fear!

Trailblazers in Motion

These clever clogs, oh what a sight,
They take on trails, both wild and slight.
In brightly colored, mismatched flair,
They set the pace without a care.

With every stomp and joyful leap,
They challenge hills that make us weep.
In socks that sparkle, soles that gleam,
Oh, what a wonderfully silly theme!

Bounding over roots, they giggle loud,
In muddy ditches, they feel so proud.
Who knew a foot could have such fun?
Skipping through sun, until day is done!

These trailblazers, quirky, bright,
With every path, they spark delight.
So here's to feet that love to roam,
In every tread, they find their home!

Beyond the Heel

When the day has just begun,
And the laces come undone,
Look beyond that little grip,
For the wild ride is just a trip!

With every wiggle, they take a stance,
Ready to hop and whirl, perchance!
Beyond the heel, there's so much to see,
Like a dance party, just for me!

They might sway and even squeak,
But that's the fun, so crazy and cheek!
In every scuff and scurry, you'll see,
Adventures waiting, wild and free.

So twirl and spin, give them a whirl,
These lively friends make hearts unfurl.
For when it comes to living life's zeal,
Let's take a leap beyond the heel!

Marks of Metamorphosis

From scuffed ol' sneakers, I take a leap,
To shiny new loafers, oh, what a creep!
Each scuff tells a tale, of battles and fights,
While the new ones just gleam, like bright city lights.

In flip-flops I ponder, my fate in a bind,
What magic exists in the soles where I grind?
With laces a-tangling, I dance with delight,
As blisters protest, claiming victory tonight!

Ascending into Fresh Terrain

With heels on the rise, I take to the sky,
But trip on my laces, oh me, oh my!
The ground comes up fast, like a long-lost friend,
I land with a thud, but I laugh till the end.

In boots made for stomping, I'm ready to play,
But mud starts to cling, in the funniest way!
Each step a new challenge, with giggles galore,
Who knew transformation could open such doors?

Ribbons of Change in the Fabric of Life

Laces like ribbons, they twist and they twirl,
Each step is like dancing, just give it a whirl!
My sandals are laughing, they're tickling my toes,
While sneakers just chuckle, as chaos bestows.

With every new pair, I embrace the absurd,
From crocs to stilettos, who needs a herd?
They say change is a journey, so pack up your flair,
And strut with a grin, for life's but a fair!

Footprints of Evolution

In old clogs I stumble, a puppet on strings,
While flashy new trainers make a fuss about bling!
Each footprint a story, a giggle in time,
As I trip on my tongue—wait, it's my rhyme!

Remember the flippers that flapped in the tide?
They taught me that joy often comes with a slide.
Each pair is a lesson, in laughter and glee,
So dance with your footprints and let them run free!

Traversing the Landscape of Hope

Each stroll brings laughter loud,
With mismatched socks, I feel so proud.
The path ahead is full of dreams,
I leap like frogs, or so it seems.

I trip on pebbles, find a groove,
My feet have skills that make me move.
In every step, a giggle hides,
Adventure awaits, oh how it glides!

My sandals squeak, my sneakers squeal,
A wobbly dance makes spirits feel.
The ground beneath may shift and sway,
But laughter leads me on my way.

So let's embrace this silly jaunt,
With every step, a playful flaunt.
Through fields and puddles, here we go,
Life's a game, let's steal the show!

Every Step a New Beginning

With every step, my laces fly,
They trip me up, oh me, oh my!
I waddle now, I bounce and skip,
My shoes do backflips, what a trip!

Each toe a rebel, breaking free,
They have their own plans, won't listen to me.
With every clunk and clatter loud,
My feet make jokes, they're quite the crowd.

I shuffle here, then leap right there,
My sneakers sing, a wild flair.
In this wacky, twisty race,
My feet just want to keep up the pace.

So here's to change, with laughter bright,
Each step a spark, a dash of light.
In this odd dance called life, it seems,
I'll follow my heart and chase my dreams!

The Dance of Unchanged Paths

Tap your toes, then spin around,
On this path, new quirks are found.
With heavy boots and flippy flops,
My feet have thoughts; they frequently stop.

A misstep here, a jig there too,
Oh look, a squirrel! What shall we do?
With tiny shakes and silly hops,
My dance is wild, it never stops.

Around the bends the laughter leads,
While my laces tangle with the weeds.
I moonwalk on this trail of fun,
Each misfit step a race begun.

So join the frolic, let's make a fuss,
No route to boring, ride the bus!
With every spin and leap we share,
A vibrant life beyond compare!

Grounded Growth

From sneakers sprout, a garden bright,
In every hole, a worm's delight.
With muddy soles and tattered seams,
I'm planting laughter, it's sprouting dreams.

The daisies giggle as I stroll,
My feet, a comedy, take the toll.
Each root I step on forms a joke,
With every bounce, the flowers stoke.

I stomp on grass like it's a mat,
And squirrels wave back — imagine that!
In this crazy patch, I take my stand,
With open toes and wiggly hands.

So come along, let's take a chance,
In mud and joy, we'll learn to dance.
With every wobble, laugh and sway,
We'll grow together, come what may!

The Art of Moving Forward

With every step, a shoe does squeak,
Yet on we strut, so chic, so peak.
The left is bold, the right unsure,
Together they dance, that's for sure.

An old sole sighs, 'I need a break!'
But the new one laughs, 'Let's awake!'
To twirl and spin, we'll find a way,
In mismatched bliss, we seize the day.

Crossover to Change

One foot slides out, the other in,
What a journey, this goofy spin.
With every flip, the ground feels new,
Oh, the blunders our soles can do!

So tripping on fate, we laugh out loud,
In bouncy colors, we stand proud.
A little twist, a wobbly cheer,
Adventures await, let's shift a gear!

Foundations of Future Paths

With soles that squeal on the dusty floor,
We pave our way, oh, what a chore!
They're laced with dreams, yet worn from time,
Each step a giggle, in silly rhyme.

Oh, the patterns that make us grin,
Stripes and polka dots, let's begin!
Kick up the dust, let's create a scene,
In every stroll, we chase the dream.

The Weight of New Beginnings

The new kicks chafe, but that's alright,
We'll shuffle around by morning light.
Though heavy with hope, they're rather spunky,
Each step's a giggle, each twist is funky.

As we stumble forth, shoes squeak and slide,
Let laughter echo, let joy be our guide.
In every trip, we're destined to rise,
For in these laughs, our spirit flies.

Steps to a Brighter Future

Some claim that new kicks bring luck,
While others think that's just plain stuck.
I strutted in bright colors bold,
Then tripped like a clown, oh behold!

In my journey to glitter and shine,
A right foot, a left foot, oh how they align!
But gravity laughed, and down I went,
Pants a bit ripped, my pride not spent!

Dancing wildly to a tune in my head,
But those flip-flops had other plans instead.
With a squeak and a squawk, I took off a toe,
A step toward the future? More like an impromptu show!

Yet through every tumble, each boisterous cheer,
I learned that the joy is what we hold dear.
So lace them up tight, let's venture ahead,
In outrageous attire, laughter's our thread!

Threads of Metamorphosis

From sneakers so new to sandals that squeal,
Each pair tells a tale, like a light-up wheel.
I wore mismatched colors to cause quite a stir,
"Fashion's an art!" I giggled, with flair to concur.

That day in the park, I trod on a bee,
Managed to shout out, "What a buzz life can be!"
With each awkward step, my confidence peeked,
My toes danced freely, my ankles quite squeaked.

The catcalls of squirrels echoed in glee,
As pigeons played judge, who's best dressed? Not me!
But laughter erupted with every toe tap,
In this circus of footwear, we're all in the lap.

Old boots give a wink as they sit on the rack,
While new kicks beg to wander, no keeping them back.
So let's skip and let slide, our hearts full of cheer,
In this merry parade, we embrace every year!

Stitches of Awakening

Once I found a pair that promised to dance,
But they tripped on my feet, crazy foot romance.
With my flats on a mission, they plotted a prank,
"One step forward, two back!" they giggled, how dank!

In a flip-flop frenzy, I soared through the air,
Yet landed like jelly, with not a care.
My high-tops rebelled, wanting to play,
"Let's jump into puddles, come what may!"

We raced down the street, like mad little sprites,
Laughing at life, forgetting wrongs and rights.
The rain started falling, but who cares tonight?
In these nutty old soles, the joy was in sight!

With each little stitch, the fun wasn't done,
For every odd pattern brings a dash of sun.
So bounce and let wiggle your toes in the light,
In this whimsical dance, we'll make the wrongs right!

The Movement Beneath

Oh, the shuffle and shuffle, the wiggle and sweep,
Came a groove in my gait that made my friends leap.
With tap shoes that clattered and boots that would funk,
The crowd roared with laughter as I slid into junk!

Wearing socks with my sandals, so daring, divine,
Who knew such a choice could cross fashion's line?
Yet out on the sidewalk, I shimmied with flair,
"Just call me the trendsetter!" I boldly declared.

But my soles had their secrets, a tendency wild,
One step on the grass made me fall like a child.
The squirrels snickered hard, the birds all had roars,
As I danced with the daisies, winning foot wars!

Through the quirky missteps, I found my own way,
With each joyful tumble, I chose to splay.
So here's to the movement, the fun and the glee,
May we all take the leap, let our passions run free!

a Continuum of Steps

In closets deep where secrets hide,
Old sneakers laugh, their tongues untied.
Each pair a tale, a dance, a spree,
Mocking the land of monotony.

The clogs are waiting, with their clatter,
While flip-flops whisper, 'What's the matter?'
With every scuff they try to share,
Miscalculated jumps, we meet the air!

The loafers sigh, proclaiming grace,
As laces fight for a binding place.
Together we march, oh what a sight,
One toe too crooked, the other too tight!

So here we bounce, from heel to toe,
Wobbling onward, with style to show.
In the journey of life let's mix and twirl,
In every step, find a silly whirl.

The Riddle of the Unworn

A pair of boots, pristine and bright,
Staring at dust, they sigh in fright.
'Why all these tags? We've never been out!'
To tread where no feet dare, they pout.

The sandals peek, 'What's this fuss?
Imagine the fun—you'll miss the bus!'
But left by the door, they still remain,
Talking of trips that they'll never gain.

The oxfords sit with a poker face,
Dreaming of dances in a grand old place.
Yet here they sit—unbuttoned, unfazed,
While dust bunnies in party hats are amazed.

Oh, the riddle of shoes that collect just dust,
Promises whispered turn to rust.
So reach for the laces, let's take a chance,
Who knows what awaits if we dare to dance?

From Dust to Destiny

A scuffed old pair with a glorious story,
Worn through the mud, they bask in glory.
From puddles and parks to fancy soirées,
They've got memories packed in the frays.

Once resting quiet in a darkened nook,
Now strutting along with a spunky look.
'Watch where you step, heed the advice,
We've traipsed where no one's dare rolled the dice!'

Each crack and crease, a comedy sketch,
With laughter echoing, their souls they fetch.
From awkward moments to joyous sparks,
They plot their journey under street lights' marks.

So grab a good pair and shake off the dust,
In every stumble, in every gust.
Embrace the weirdness, with purpose and glee,
From dust we rise, in quirky harmony!

Steps That Bind Us

A mismatched pair, a tale of two,
One's lived in luxury, the other in goo.
Together they wander, a sight quite rare,
In this tango of life, they dance with flair.

The galoshes giggle, while leather boots strut,
'Where are you from? Your mud? So gross!'
Yet each step sparks laughter, tensions erased,
In the rhythm of soles, they joyfully faced.

Patched-up old sneakers, chattering bright,
'Tiara of thorns, or a crown of delight?'
They hop through the puddles, a leap of faith,
Creating a bond, defying the wraith.

So here's to the mishaps, the laughter, the spins,
In the steps we take, the fun never thins.
For in each sole's journey, a story rings true,
In the dance we embark—oh, how we grew!

Horizons Underfoot

Worn-out soles on a bright blue path,
Tap dance with the chaos, feel the laugh.
Each step a story, a twist, a twirl,
In silly sneakers, we joyfully swirl.

Oh, the adventures on these quirky feet,
Dodging puddles, finding rhythm in the street.
With every stumble, we giggle and glide,
In this bouncy journey, we take in stride.

Echoes in the Tread

Have you heard the whispers beneath my kicks?
They chatter and gossip, sharing all their tricks.
Each scuff and scrape tells a tale of delight,
From dance-offs to mishaps, day turns to night.

Tiptoeing past the gumball and the grime,
My soles make music, a hilarious rhyme.
In this quirky rhythm, we'll skip and we'll prance,
Join in the fun, take a chance on this dance!

Ascending with Each Footfall

Up, up we go with a hop and a skip,
Mountains of laughter, let's take a trip.
My laces are tangled, a knotty affair,
But watch how I conquer with flair in the air!

With every footfall, the world seems to grin,
Silly mischief always bubbles within.
Balancing life on my wobbly toes,
In the circus of living, let's strike a pose!

Reimagining the Step

A twist to the left, now shimmy to the right,
With fancies and flops, we create pure delight.
These playful strides lead us to the unknown,
In the game of the soles, we're kings on the throne!

So here's to the moments that make us all smile,
In this wild wonderland, let's stay for a while.
Every hop is a giggle, every jab a cheer,
With sneakers of laughter, we'll wander far, my dear!

Footprints in the Fabric of Time

In a world of mismatched pairs,
Dancing round with silly stares,
Each step a giggle, what a sight,
As we strut beneath the moonlight.

With every mark upon the ground,
There's laughter in the echoes, found.
A trail of joy wherever we roam,
Our path of whimsy feels like home.

The clocks tick loud, but we don't care,
In playful leaps, we float like air.
The journey's wise, the journey's bright,
With every twist, we're feeling light.

Bouncing back like rubber bands,
Creating chaos while life stands.
With each footprint, a tale to tell,
In fabric woven, all is well.

The Dance of Progress

Twirl around in polished flair,
Shuffle steps with a funny pair.
Moonwalk forward, then backward slide,
As we giggle, our strides collide.

Progress hops on tippy toes,
Waltzing where curiosity grows.
Round and round, we spin with glee,
Each misstep sings, 'Come dance with me!'

With every beat, we break the mold,
Funky moves that never get old.
Rhythms mix like colors bright,
In this curious, silly fight.

So sway and shake, let laughter reign,
In this joyous, happy train.
Each dance a sign that we're alive,
With every jig, together we thrive.

Laces Untied

Laces flapping in the breeze,
Trip and stumble with such ease.
Tied in knots that just won't stay,
Laughing hard as they sway away.

The world's our stage, we tumble down,
Wearing giggles like a crown.
As loops and ribbons interlace,
We embrace our silly grace.

A dash to the left, a slip to the right,
With untied dreams, we take flight.
Every kick a chance to play,
In this wild and carefree ballet.

With laces loose, we skip and slide,
Fueled by laughter, joy our guide.
Each hop a promise of delight,
In the chaos, we find our light.

Dreams Aligned

In a line of quirky shoes,
Everyone picks their own muse.
Whispers of dreams tucked in the soles,
As we gather, each heart rolls.

The oddest styles, mismatched views,
Brave to dance in polka dots or blues.
Strutting proudly with a wink,
Life's a canvas, let's paint and link.

That shuffle shuffle, hip-hop sound,
Moves made only by the profound.
As we glide through life's parade,
Our mismatched steps never fade.

With dreams aligned and spirits high,
Together we'll reach for the sky.
In our own rhythm, no need to fear,
Each laugh we share, a dream so dear.

Stride into Tomorrow's Light

Striding forth in colors bold,
Each footstep a new tale told.
With enthusiasm painting the air,
Every hop whispers, 'Why not dare?'

Tomorrow's light a gleaming glow,
Guides our path where silly winds blow.
We skip, we hop, we dance with zest,
In this game, we're truly blessed.

With every stride, the world reshapes,
Inventing giggles, bending drapes.
The future's bright in every sway,
In our playful hearts, come what may.

So lace up laughter, set your sights,
In vibrant dreams, we'll find our rights.
Join the playful parade, take part,
Stride boldly forth, let joy be art.

The Dance of Change

In sneakers bright, I twirl and spin,
A tumble here, oh where to begin?
With every step, my toes declare,
Let's kick it up, I haven't a care!

The sandals squeak, a summer tune,
They tango down to the light of the moon.
With laces tied, I leap so high,
I might just touch the cotton candy sky!

Imprints of Innovation

My loafers laugh with every stride,
They wiggle quick and take great pride.
Creative soles, a funny feat,
Each step a giggle, oh what a treat!

The high-tops hop, they love to play,
They bounce and bounce, then fly away.
With colors bold, and patterns wild,
These wacky prints have my inner child!

Marching Towards Tomorrow

In mismatched socks, I take a stand,
With colorful kicks, a lively band.
They stomp and march, no need to pout,
As they parade, the doubts fade out!

Each step a joke, with laughter loud,
Together we dance, a happy crowd.
Oh what a sight, as we all prance,
In quirky shoes, we find our chance!

The Fabric of Footwear

In slippers soft, I shuffle slow,
A lazy loop, like a gentle flow.
With every squish, a giggle breaks,
Oh, how these fuzzy friends can shake!

The boots I wear, they clomp with glee,
Each stomp a story, wild and free.
Oh what a tale, this fabric weaves,
Of running errands and autumn leaves!

Pathways of Progress

On sidewalks where my feet conspire,
Each step ignites my heart's desire.
With laces tied in silly knots,
I dance through life, forget the spots.

A leap to lunch, I trip so bold,
Past hotdog stands and tales retold.
My soles may squeak like mice on cheese,
But laughter's what my spirit sees.

Through puddles deep, I make a splash,
My shoes your standard, just a trash.
With squeaky shoes, I rule the crowd,
A jester's heart, forever loud.

So let my worn-out soles declare,
Each misstep's right, in light of flair.
As I navigate this joyful maze,
Progress comes in quirky ways.

The Journey Beneath

Upon my feet, these lumpy quirks,
They bounce around like clueless jerks.
They wiggle left, they wobble right,
A waltz of chaos, pure delight!

Each step I take's a chance to trip,
Spontaneous dance, a silly skip.
With holes that tell of time and place,
They've led me on a wild goose chase.

In crowded trains, they push and shove,
A mosh pit of mismatched love.
Yet through the noise, a giggle snuck,
Should I wear socks that don't quite pluck?

So here I go, the world is wide,
With every bend, my fears subside.
Where funny tricks are all the rage,
It's just my path, my stage, my page.

Strides of Renewal

With boots that squeak and sneakers torn,
I stomp around, I'm never worn.
In neon colors, oh what a sight,
I strut like peacocks, oh what a flight!

My sandals flop, my loafers squeal,
In wobbly grace, I spin the wheel.
They take me where the giggles flow,
To cheeky spots, I'm in the know.

Each flashy step a brand new chance,
The world awaits a wild dance.
So join me now, let's jiggle free,
With every step, let's simply be!

The journey's fun, it starts anew,
In zany paths, we'll wander through.
With laughter echoing in the breeze,
We skip along with hearts of ease.

Laces of Liberation

Tangled laces, oh what a mess,
They're my companions, no need to stress.
With every fumble, chaos reigns,
Yet in this spectacle, joy remains.

From cobblestone streets to grassy fields,
They guide my feet, their mystery yields.
Who needs a map when my shoes can show,
The hidden wonders of life's grand show?

With laughter echoing out so loud,
My shoes tap out, they're bold and proud.
In puddles deep, they splash like mad,
Creating ripples, making me glad.

So here's to laces that break the mold,
With every journey, new stories told.
In the frenzy of life, we'll find our fate,
Through goofy steps, we celebrate!

Footsteps of Transformation

Old kicks on my feet, they squeak and they squawk,
Trying to impress with my funky sock talk.
Every step's a slip, a trip and a fall,
My laces are tangled, oh dear, that's my call.

The neighbors all stare, they burst out in glee,
With a graceful twirl, I knock over a tree.
But a dance like my dad gives me hope for the best,
In these quirky old shoes, I've found my new zest.

I strut through the park, bold and unafraid,
My footwork's a magic show, plans I've made.
No need for a mirror, they get in the way,
Just show off my moves—it's the wobbly sway.

So here's to the steps, both forward and back,
My soles have a story, they're never off track.
With each little stumble, a lesson I'll find,
In the shoes of my choices, I'm truly aligned.

Soles of New Beginnings

A pair once pristine, now in need of repair,
I laugh at their fate, it's a comical affair.
They've walked through the mud, they've jumped in the snow,
Yet still, they tell tales of the places we go.

Worn down on the edges, but full of great cheer,
Every scuff and bump holds a memory dear.
At the coffee shop, I make quite the scene,
As my flip-flops go flapping, it's the soles' dance routine!

I tried on some sneakers that looked oh-so-smooth,
But with a loud squeak, it's my charm that they lose.
A stutter-step shuffle, a twist and a glide,
With laces like spaghetti, I just cannot hide.

Yet laughter erupts with each quirky mishap,
A tumble, a trip, oh look, now a nap!
In these untamed travels, my spirit runs free,
With soles underfoot, who knows where I'll be?

Steps Through Unfamiliar Paths

Adventure awaits, but wait—what's that smell?
Did my shoes just complain? Oh, all's well!
I tread on the path where the wild daisies grow,
My foot's not quite sure where it wants to go.

Around every corner, there's mischief and fun,
With every misplaced step, giggles are spun.
A leap in the puddle, I land with a splash,
These shoes of mine wobble, but they're quite the rash!

From cobblestones worn to the soft sandy shore,
Each footprint I leave is a tale to explore.
With a skip and a hop, I raise up a cheer,
No maps on my feet, just a heart full of fear!

So bring on the distance, the dirt, and the mud,
My footsteps will tell of the times I have slid.
With a laugh and a wobble, I'm proud as can be,
In the dance of the odd, I'm forever set free!

The Journey Beneath Our Feet

The journey begins with a shimmer and shine,
But wait, is that grass? Oh no, that's a vine!
With sneakers that squeak and sand in between,
My toes are in trouble; they're making a scene.

Each step is a riddle, a puzzle to solve,
In these rubbery traps, my patience evolves.
A tiptoe on carpet, a slide down the hall,
Then BAM! I almost lost it! Oh, I'm having a ball.

I wear mismatched socks, it's my own special flair,
While my shoes seem to bicker and argue—oh dear!
But with each silly stumble, I thrive and I thrive,
In this wacky grand show, I'm just glad I'm alive!

So here's to the journeys and each little beat,
With laughter and charm, let's give life a treat.
In this puzzle of steps, I'll dance with delight,
With my feet ever ready for mischief tonight!

Soles that Whisper of Destiny

In a closet so full, there's a shoe for each day,
Yet they somehow conspire, to lead me astray.
With a flip here and there, they giggle and chatter,
"Where'll you go next? Let's see what's the matter!"

Oh, the loafers I bought for a fancy affair,
Decided themselves for a race through the air.
With a squeak and a squelch, they jumped from the shelf,
And I chased after them, forgetting myself!

Those heels that seemed sturdy, ready for flair,
Tripped on my dreams, now I'm stuck in despair.
They're laughing so hard, as I tumble and roll,
"You wanted a dance? How about a stroll!"

As I pick up the pairs that made such a mess,
I wonder if they plot for my own happiness.
With soles full of secrets, they twist, twirl, and sway,
Maybe they just want to dance me away!

A Canvas of Changing Journeys

Each morning I wake with a wild little scheme,
While my sandals conspire, plotting a dream.
They tell me with glee, as they stretch in the sun,
"Let's hike up a hill, and we'll see who can run!"

There's a sneaker so bright, says, "I've seen it all!"
While the dress shoe just sighs, "I prefer the ball."
But the crocs throw a fit, let out a loud croak,
"Why follow the rules? Let's just go for a soak!"

I try to decide, but they put on a show,
With a shimmy, a shake, they steal all the glow.
"The park or the beach? Which adventure to seize?"
They bicker and wrestle as I struggle to please.

At last, I just laugh, and I set them all free,
"You can come along, but you're all in a spree!"
Off we trot together, a colorful crew,
Painting paths in the world, oh, what fun we'll do!

The Weight of Each Step Forward

Step by step, oh what a scene,
With laces untied and soles in between.
I hoped for a trot, but I slipped and I slid,
My dad's old shoes just laughed, what a way to be rid!

My boots declared war on the muddy terrain,
"Every leap you take just adds to the gain!"
Yet they sunk like anchors, while the sneakers just soared,

"You're weighing us down! With each step, we're floored!"

A flip-flop chimed in with a twang and a fling,
"Why care about weight? Let's just dance and sing!"
I tried to keep balance, but it sent me off track,
With laughter the chorus, I can't hold them back!

As I landed face-first, my shoes cheered "Hooray!"
They've swapped my ambitions for a funny ballet.
In the weight of each step, I found joy in the fall,
With my soles all a-grinning, it was worth it after all!

Beyond the Comfort of Familiar Paths

In the cupboard they groan, some too cozy to leave,
"Why wander the world? We've got all we believe!"
But one little slipper, with a spark in its thread,
Whispered, "Let's take risks, let's go where we've fled!"

We ventured outside, the grass felt so strange,
As the boots took a wobble, I thought, "What a change!"
"Feel that breeze, oh dear friends, it's a wild, wild ride!"
While the loafers sat tight, "We prefer to abide!"

The sandals rolled over, "Let's dance on the rocks!"
While the dress shoe just yelled, "These are no fancy flocks!"
But the novelty tickled, as we shimmied and spun,
Turning fear into laughter, oh my, weren't we fun!

So off we all went, with a wiggle and cheer,
Beyond these sweet walls, let's embrace the sincere.
And though some will stay, snug and warm in the dark,
We'll venture to places that ignite the heart's spark!

Treads of Tomorrow's Dreams

Lace them up, let's have some fun,
Each step's a dance, we've just begun.
With every stomp, new paths will sprout,
In mismatched pairs, we'll laugh and shout.

Bouncing here, tripping there,
Why worry if our style's rare?
A little squeak with every stride,
In goofy kicks, we'll take great pride!

Mud on toes, grass in our laces,
Life's a game in wild places.
We'll leap and twirl, catch the breeze,
With crazy shoes, we aim to please!

So tie them tight and let's explore,
With every step, we crave for more.
In funky kicks, our spirits gleam,
We're the stars of tomorrow's dream!

Worn with Purpose

Two left feet or one right shoe,
Walking funny, but hey, who knew?
With holes and scuffs, we strut our stuff,
These quirky pairs are just enough.

Frayed at the edges, we start to glide,
In these old kicks, we'll show our pride.
Life's a circus, we're the clowns,
In worn-out gear, we'll flip the frowns.

The squeaky sound is our parade,
With every step, new memories made.
In mismatched pairs, we find our groove,
Dance like no one's watching, let's move!

So let it rain or let it shine,
Our silly steps are grand divine.
With purpose clear and joy in tow,
In funny shoes, we steal the show!

The Canvas of Change

Painted soles with colors bright,
Every step, a stroke of light.
We'll sashay through puddles and mud,
Creating art – it's just our thud!

A splash of red, a dash of blue,
Who needs a brush when you've got two?
In patterns wild, we march in style,
Our feet are canvases all the while.

With every print, we make a scene,
In funky hues, we reign supreme.
Let's leave our mark, it's quite a show,
In painted kicks, watch us glow!

So grab some paint, and let's not wait,
Transforming paths, it's not too late.
With laughter loud, let's be bold,
Our canvas shines in every fold!

Push Forward

One step, two steps, a little hop,
With silly dancing, we can't be stopped.
Through bustling streets, we'll zig and zag,
In rubber soles that make us brag!

Kick the air, embrace the sway,
In bouncy shoes, we laugh and play.
Let's twirl it out, spin around,
In funky feet, we're joyfully bound.

With every leap, we touch the sky,
No looking back, we spread our wings wide.
In rubber bands and shimmery toes,
We'll storm the world, everyone knows!

So let's step forth, don't hesitate,
With rhythm and beat, oh, it's our fate!
In jubilant strides, we dance through life,
With every push, we conquer strife!

Step Strong

Silly soles that make a sound,
With every step, we shake the ground.
In bright blue hues or neon green,
Watch us strut like you've never seen!

A little wobble, a tiny sway,
In joyful chaos, we find our way.
With every stomp, we laugh and cheer,
In zany kicks, we shed all fear!

From sneakers loud to boots with flair,
We leave our mark everywhere.
A twirl, a jump, let's make it grand,
In funny shoes, we'll take a stand!

So step it out, embrace the beat,
In this silly dance, we find our feet.
With every giggle, we carry along,
On this wacky path, we step so strong!

The Journey Woven into Every Tread

In a world where soles get scuffed,
My closet's full of dreams quite tough.
Each step a giggle, every leap a laugh,
Just hope they fit — no photograph!

From flip-flops to boots, I've tried them all,
Stumbling like a toddler, yet I stand tall.
The sneakers laugh as I trip and slide,
Join me in this chaotic ride!

Worn-out sandals with stories to share,
Of dance-offs and stumbles done without care.
Each tread tells tales of laughter and glee,
As mismatched pairs roam wild and free!

So here's to roads both twisty and bent,
With friends at hand and time well spent.
Unlace those troubles, run wild and bright,
In joyous steps, let's dance through the night!

Unbound Walks, Uncharted Dreams

Take a step, trip on a twig,
In sneakers so bright, I'm feeling so big.
Wobbling paths with a giggle or two,
I'm like a colt, but without a clue!

Two left feet and a very loose lace,
The world becomes my grand playground space.
With every tumble, I just grin wide,
Exploring like a puppy, tail held with pride.

Stride through puddles, a splash and a cheer,
That murky water? Now, that's a souvenir!
My soles are a map, each mark is a friend,
In laughter we wander, no need to pretend.

So let's roam together, through rain or through shine,
In this unbound journey, it's sass that's divine.
Forget the GPS, let the good times roll,
With every misstep, we're owning our stroll!

Navigating the Terrain of Transformation

With each new dawn, I lace up to prance,
In this quirky ballet of chance and romance.
Leaping across cracks and dodging the grind,
Who needs a map when you've got the blind?

I shuffle, I skip, like a human pogo,
In a whirl of colors, I'm quite the show!
My arch isn't great, but hey, that's the plan,
To dance through the blunders, like only I can!

Every footwear's got a tale to tell,
From rubbery rain boots to those that yell.
Those slippers may frown, but oh, they love me,
Embracing the chaos, setting dreams free.

So buckle that lace, embark on the ride,
Unraveling wonders as we glide side by side.
In this playful expedition, let laughter blend,
Finding joy in the jumbles, on that, we depend!

Trails of Renewal

I traipse through life with my toes in the air,
Chasing these whims like I haven't a care.
In tattered old flats, I prance and I play,
Who knew a shoe could turn into a ballet?

From bouncing in boots to sliding in slips,
I chase after dreams sans any scripts.
Each puddle's a portal, a splash, and a spree,
Sweet laughter and chaos, come dance along with me!

My journey's a cycle where funny meets fun,
Sometimes I trip, but I never quite run.
With snares of old laces and heels out of place,
I float on these trails, with a smile on my face.

Together we'll forge paths that sparkle and shine,
In sidewalks of laughter, our destinies twine.
Jump into adventures, let stories unfurl,
In these trails of renewal, let joy be our pearl!

Tread Lightly

Step by step, what a hop,
I'm wearing sandals made of pop.
Each footfall is a little song,
With squeaks and squawks, can't go wrong.

If I stumble, don't you fret,
These silly soles are my best bet.
They tickle toes and wiggle cheer,
I'll dance away without a fear.

The pavement's tough, but my soles are spry,
They bounce along, oh me, oh my!
I might look clumsy, it's true I do,
But these giggly shoes know just what's due.

So tread lightly on this goofy track,
With every step, just don't look back.
In funny shoes, let's skip and sway,
Embrace the fun, come what may.

Grow Boldly

Oh, my friends, let's take the plunge,
In flashy kicks, we'll boldly lunge.
With colors bright and patterns wild,
We'll strut our stuff, just like a child.

Each step we take a brand-new quest,
In shoes so loud, you'll be impressed.
The world's our stage, so let's perform,
With every stomp, we'll break the norm.

Forget the rules, let's jump and spin,
In these zany shoes, we'll always win.
Through puddles deep or mud so slick,
Our feet are fearless, that's the trick!

So wear them proud, and wear them loud,
In every crowd, we'll stand unbowed.
With every stride, let laughter flow,
In shoes that dance, we steal the show!

Echoes of Evolving Soles

In these whirly kicks, I glide with care,
Like a peacock's tail, I strut and flare.
They squeak and squeal, a vocal pack,
With every step, there's no turning back.

From alleyways to busy streets,
My shoes leave tales of clumsy feats.
A slip, a slide, a wild cha-cha,
Oh, how I wish I was a ballerina!

Each day they morph, they twist and twine,
Every scuff a mark, a life divine.
With squeaky notes that fill the air,
In evolving soles, we dance—oh, rare!

So if you hear my shoes' parade,
Join in the fun, don't be afraid.
For in this wacky, joyful roll,
We find the magic in every soul.

Paths Worn with Purpose

On paths I wander, soles a-flap,
With every footprint, let the giggles map.
The road is long but filled with cheer,
These scuffed-up shoes have no hint of fear.

With every misstep, a tale unfolds,
In wobbling shoes, adventure holds.
Slipping and sliding, I laugh out loud,
In these quirky trails, I'm oh so proud.

Pavement, grass, or mud so thick,
My shoes embrace every little trick.
Through puddles, streams, and sunny rays,
We'll stomp our way through life's wild maze.

So here's to paths we boldly take,
In silly shoes for laughter's sake.
Each journey a dance, each slip a chance,
Let's twirl and whirl in the shoe parade dance!

Sandals of a Shifting Landscape

With colors bright, my sandals sway,
Through shifting sands, I spin and play.
A little left, a little right,
In blaze of laughter, I take flight.

Each grain of sand tells tales of fun,
In funky clogs that weigh a ton.
If I trip, I'll just laugh it off,
In these wild things, can't help but scoff.

Through rocky trails and grass so green,
My wobbling ways are quite a scene.
With every step, the world's my stage,
In colorful wear, I turn the page.

So join my dance, come laugh with me,
In sandals bright, we'll roam so free.
Together we'll make the best of trends,
With twinkling feet, we'll ride the bends.

Transformation Underfoot

Old kicks in the closet, they sit and they sigh,
Waiting for the chance to give life a try.
With a squeak and a wiggle, they dance in delight,
Planning their journey under the moonlight.

Laces like snakes, they tangle and twist,
Every hop and a stumble, they dream of a tryst.
New paths to explore, they swell with the thrill,
Ready to conquer each bump and each hill.

A puddle appears, oh what a surprise,
With a leap and a splash, they're blurring the skies.
They giggle and chatter, with every jump made,
Creating a ruckus, a goofy parade.

Onward they march, these whimsical feet,
Dancing with whimsy, they skip to the beat.
Each step a new joke, they laugh as they roam,
Transforming the world, in their funny foam.

Grounded in Growth

Beneath my feet, the world is alive,
In sneakers so old, my spirit will thrive.
They squeak like a chorus in perfect delight,
As I twist and I turn, dancing in sunlight.

These boots are so silly, they wobble and sway,
Chasing the clouds, come what may.
With every weird bounce, they make me feel bold,
In these funky old shoes, I'm never too old.

When I trip over nothing, they giggle with glee,
"Come on, let's run, come laugh here with me!"
Each stumble a story, each trip just a jest,
In my zany old footwear, I'm always the best.

Treading on dreams that glitter and gleam,
In these whacky old soles, I'm living the dream.
Grounded in laughter, I prance and I play,
With shoes made for joy, I'm spry every day.

Footprints of the Future

Little footprints follow where I take flight,
Leaving behind giggles, a whimsical sight.
In my froggy galoshes, I hop like a clown,
Splashing through puddles, I never feel down.

Each step is a riddle, each stride a surprise,
With wobbly toes and the bluest skies.
I'm racing with shadows that tickle my feet,
In bright yellow flip-flops, life's oh-so-sweet.

Tripping on rainbows, I'm not scared to fall,
In my playful old runners, I'm having a ball.
Making fun footprints wherever I roam,
Navigating life in my happy home.

From squishy mud puddles to beaches of sand,
These zany old shoes always lend me a hand.
Each print leads to laughter, my echoing cheer,
In the quest for tomorrow, I'm spinning in gear.

A New Bounce in Every Step

A summer of sprinkles, a dash of pure fun,
My quirky old sneakers are ready to run.
Bouncing through blossoms, I twirl in delight,
Laces unruly, a slapstick flight.

Each leap is a giggle, each hop brings a cheer,
They wiggle with joy as I glide without fear.
With every odd shuffle, I break into dance,
In my playful old shoes, life's all about chance.

They're frayed at the seams, but oh what a crew,
Ready to prance in the morning dew.
With quirky adventures that go round and round,
These shoes of mine always know how to bound.

Walking on air, in a comical way,
They bounce with my laughter, come join in the play.
So here's to my footwear, forever my friend,
With a spring in my step, let the fun never end!